Who Is
Derek Jeter?

Who Is Derek Jeter?

by Gail Herman
illustrated by Andrew Thomson

Grosset & Dunlap
An Imprint of Penguin Random House

For Jeff, a Yankee and Jeter fan.
And for Sam, a Jeter fan—GH

To Rhia, for the support—AT

GROSSET & DUNLAP
Penguin Young Readers Group
An Imprint of Penguin Random House LLC

Text copyright © 2015 by Gail Herman. Illustrations copyright © 2015 by Penguin Random House LLC. All rights reserved. Published by Grosset & Dunlap, an imprint of Penguin Random House LLC, 345 Hudson Street, New York, New York 10014. Who HQ™ and all related logos are trademarks owned by Penguin Random House LLC. GROSSET & DUNLAP is a trademark of Penguin Random House LLC. Printed in the USA.

Library of Congress Cataloging-in-Publication Data is available.

ISBN 978-0-448-48697-0   10 9 8 7 6

Contents

Who Is
Derek Jeter?

On April 2, 1996, Major League Baseball's Opening Day, the New York Yankees faced the Cleveland Indians. Once, the Yankees had been the top ball club in the country. They were a dynasty, with World Series titles. But the Yankees hadn't won a championship in eighteen years. They hadn't won the American League pennant since 1981. Maybe this would be the start of a championship season at last.

Today they were playing at Cleveland's Jacobs Field, and the score was tied, 0–0, in the top of the second. The Yankees had two men on base. New York fans grew excited.

But now there were two outs. Could the Yankees still score? Twenty-one-year-old Derek Jeter

stepped to the plate. And he . . .
struck out.

Derek was the first Yankees rookie to start at
shortstop on Opening Day in more than thirty
years. *Why Derek?* some fans wondered. *Why now?*
He'd had a poor spring training. They doubted
his strength at bat and on the field. It seemed they
might be right.

Derek told himself it was okay. This was just a game like any other. He tried not to be nervous. But it was hard. He was young and inexperienced. An April Fool's snowstorm had pushed the game back a day. The wait made it even harder. But Derek was determined to make a difference.

In the fifth inning, he got a second chance at bat.

Derek took two pitches, both balls. Then he saw a high fastball. He swung. *Crack!* The ball sailed high into the left-field stands. A home run!

Two innings later, Derek made an over-the-shoulder, one-handed catch.

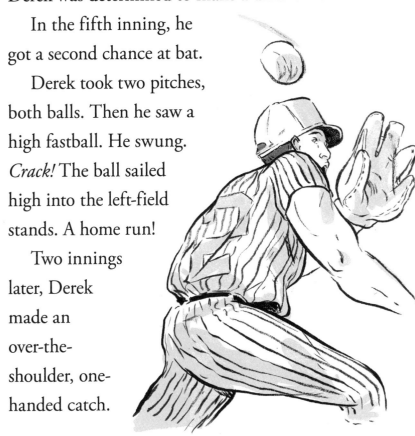

He stranded a man on base to leave the Indians scoreless. The Yankees wound up winning 7–1.

Any doubts about Derek Jeter vanished. For the Yankees, it *was* the start of a championship season. And for Derek Jeter, it was the start of an amazing major league career. By the time Derek retired, he had won five World Series titles, five Gold Gloves, five Silver Sluggers, Rookie of the Year, and a slew of other awards. He'd been a Yankee for almost half his life. And before he was a Yankee, he was a Yankees fan. Surely the biggest Yankees fan from Kalamazoo, Michigan.

YANKEES HISTORY

LOVE THEM OR HATE THEM, EVERYONE KNOWS THE YANKEES. THEY ARE ONE OF THE MOST SUCCESSFUL TEAMS IN ALL OF PRO SPORTS. AS OF 2014, THE TEAM HAD WON FORTY AMERICAN LEAGUE PENNANTS AND TWENTY-SEVEN WORLD SERIES CHAMPION- SHIPS, MORE THAN TWICE THE NUMBER OF ANY OTHER MAJOR LEAGUE TEAM. IN 1923, THE TEAM MOVED TO ITS OWN STADIUM IN THE BRONX. THAT SAME YEAR, BABE RUTH LED THE YANKEES TO THEIR FIRST WORLD SERIES CHAMPIONSHIP. MANY MORE TITLES FOLLOWED, THANKS

MICKEY MANTLE

TO LEGENDARY PLAYERS LIKE LOU GEHRIG, JOE DIMAGGIO, MICKEY MANTLE—AND DEREK JETER!

Chapter 1
Always a Yankee

Derek Sanderson Jeter grew up in Michigan. But he was born, on June 26, 1974, in Pequannock, New Jersey. He and his parents lived in nearby West Milford, close to his mom's family. Their town was just a car ride away from New York City and Yankee Stadium.

Derek's grandmother Dot was a huge Yankees fan. She grew up listening to games on the radio, cheering baseball greats Babe Ruth, Lou Gehrig, and Joe DiMaggio. She even waited on line for hours to pay her respects to Ruth when he died and his body was on view at Yankee Stadium.

YANKEES LEGENDS

BABE RUTH (FEBRUARY 6, 1895–AUGUST 16, 1948)

GEORGE HERMAN RUTH JR. BEGAN HIS BASEBALL CAREER AS A PITCHER FOR THE RED SOX. IN 1920, HE WAS TRADED TO THE YANKEES. HE PLAYED OUTFIELD AND BECAME A SLUGGING SENSATION, BREAKING HIS OWN SINGLE-SEASON HOME-RUN RECORD THREE TIMES. HIS 1927 RECORD OF SIXTY HOME RUNS STOOD FOR THIRTY-FOUR YEARS. RUTH WAS A YANKEE FOR FIFTEEN YEARS AND MADE NEWSPAPER HEADLINES FOR HIS OUTSIZE PERSONALITY, AS WELL AS HIS SKILL. HE WAS AN ORIGINAL MEMBER OF THE BASEBALL HALL OF FAME, ELECTED IN 1936.

LOU GEHRIG (JUNE 19, 1903–JUNE 2, 1941)

GEHRIG, A BORN-AND-BRED NEW YORKER AND A YANKEE FROM 1923 TO 1939, PLAYED WITH RUTH FOR TWELVE YEARS. WHILE RUTH GOT MOST OF THE HEADLINES, GEHRIG IS ALSO CONSIDERED ONE OF THE BEST PLAYERS EVER, AND ONE OF THE MOST RESPECTED. HE RETIRED IN 1939,

WHEN HE WAS DIAGNOSED WITH A FATAL ILLNESS, ALS, NOW KNOWN AS LOU GEHRIG'S DISEASE. HIS FAREWELL SPEECH INCLUDED THESE FAMOUS WORDS: "TODAY, I CONSIDER MYSELF THE LUCKIEST MAN ON THE FACE OF THIS EARTH." HE DIED ABOUT TWO YEARS LATER, KEEPING HIS YANKEES CAPTAIN TITLE UNTIL THE END.

JOE DIMAGGIO (NOVEMBER 25, 1914–MARCH 8, 1999)

DIMAGGIO PLAYED WITH GEHRIG FOR OVER THREE YEARS AS A YANKEES CENTER FIELDER. HE WAS KNOWN FOR HIS STYLE AND GRACE ON AND OFF THE FIELD. THE YANKEES' MANAGER CALLED HIM "THE MOST COMPLETE BALLPLAYER I'VE EVER SEEN." HIS RECORD FIFTY–SIX–GAME HITTING STREAK IN 1941 STILL STANDS.

When Derek was four, his family moved
to Kalamazoo, Michigan. His dad, Charles, a
social worker, was going back to college to get
another degree. His mom, named Dot like his
grandmother, planned to work as an accountant.

The move wasn't easy. At first, Charles and
Dot couldn't find a place to live. Landlords
wouldn't rent to them. Why?

Charles was black and Dot was white.

Derek's dad had grown up in Alabama with his mother and four sisters. Back then in the South, black people lived in a separate world from white people. It wasn't by choice. It was how white people wanted it. They wanted to keep black people apart—or segregated. Charles had to go to all-black schools, drink from water fountains that were for blacks only, and eat at different restaurants than whites.

Dot, from New Jersey, had a big family, with thirteen brothers and sisters. She met Charles in Germany, when they were in the US Army, and fell in love. Not long after, they decided to marry.

Every summer, the Jeters took Derek and his younger sister, Sharlee, to visit their grandparents. Their aunts, uncles, and cousins were all big Yankees fans. Derek became a fan, too. He already loved baseball—just like his dad.

Derek knew that Charles had played shortstop
in college. He'd seen his dad's scrapbook filled
with photos. And he watched his father play
softball games in Kalamazoo. Derek wanted to be
like his father. So as soon as he could, he joined a
T-ball league.

Derek couldn't get enough of the game. He wanted to catch, throw, and hit whenever he could. For years, he'd try on his uniform the night before a game and parade around the house, checking himself in every mirror.

When Derek was six, Grandma Dot took
him to Yankee Stadium. It looked bigger than
anything he'd ever seen. *What would it be like to
be a Yankee?* he wondered.

Kalamazoo wasn't far from Detroit and Tiger Stadium. So back home in Michigan, Charles took Derek to see the Yankees play the Tigers. Of course Derek rooted for New York. Charles, though, cheered on the Tigers.

Growing up, Derek's father had hated the Yankees. The team was one of the last all-white ball clubs. They didn't hire a black player until 1955. That was eight years after Jackie Robinson broke baseball's color barrier.

JACKIE ROBINSON

Derek admired his dad and wanted to be like him. That's why he played shortstop. But he wasn't going to stop rooting for the Yankees. He'd seen them play, on TV and in person. And they were just so exciting to watch. Derek had a poster of his favorite player, Dave Winfield, hanging on his bedroom wall. He always wore Yankees jerseys, baseball caps, and jackets.

Derek was a Yankees fan, through and through.

ELSTON HOWARD
(FEBRUARY 23, 1929–DECEMBER 14, 1980)

HOWARD WAS THE FIRST AFRICAN AMERICAN TO JOIN THE YANKEES. HE GREW UP IN ST. LOUIS, MISSOURI, PLAYED IN THE ALL-BLACK NEGRO LEAGUES, THEN MADE HIS NEW YORK DEBUT IN 1955. HE WAS A YANKEE FOR TWELVE YEARS, UNTIL HE WAS TRADED TO THE RED SOX, AND A NINE-TIME ALL-STAR, WITH TWO GOLD GLOVES FOR CATCHING. IN 1963 HE MADE HISTORY AS THE FIRST BLACK PLAYER TO WIN THE AMERICAN LEAGUE MVP AWARD. HE RETURNED TO THE YANKEES AS FIRST-BASE COACH, AND HIS NUMBER, 32, IS RETIRED.

Chapter 2
Major League Dreams

When the Jeters first moved to Michigan, they lived in an apartment complex. Derek's friends would bike over to play baseball. They'd head to a grassy area everyone called Derek Jeter's hill, because he was out there so often.

Derek would get as many kids together as he could. Younger, older, boy, girl—he didn't care. He was all about baseball.

One night, Derek went to his parents' room and made an announcement: He was going to play for the New York Yankees.

Derek was a skinny eight-year-old. He was wearing pajamas. He didn't look anything like a major league ballplayer. But his parents listened carefully.

They explained what it would take for it to happen. That Derek would be competing with athletes from all over the world. And even though he was a top player in his Little League, the other players would be top players, too.

Derek knew he'd have to work hard. And he understood about competition. He and his dad played games all the time. Checkers. Card games.

They even watched TV game shows together, guessing at answers. Charles never played badly just to let Derek win. Derek had to win fair and square.

When Derek was ten and visiting New Jersey, he learned more about hard work. His grandpa Sonny took him to his job one day. Just like Sonny always did, they woke up at 4:30 in the morning.

Sonny took care of a church and school. He painted walls, made repairs, and kept everything in shape.

When Derek got out of the car, it was hot and muggy. Mosquitoes buzzed all around. Sonny led him to the football field. Derek's job: to mow the grass.

The grass came up to Derek's knees. And the lawn mower didn't have a motor. Small, skinny Derek had to push it back and forth, back and forth. It took all his strength.

For six hours, Derek mowed the field. He
sweated. He ached. But he kept going. When
he was done, he felt proud. He finished the job
all by himself. But he realized something. If he
was going to work that hard, he'd much rather
be doing something he enjoyed . . . like playing
baseball.

About that same time, Derek's family moved to
their first house. It was right behind the public high
school, Kalamazoo Central. Derek could climb
the backyard fence and use all the school fields.

In fact, the whole family would hop the fence to play baseball and softball. Sharlee was shaping up to be a star softball shortstop.

As for Derek, he played soccer, tennis, and basketball. But baseball was his passion.

Charles and Dot went to every game they could. They went to school events and parent-teacher conferences, too. In fact, Derek's parents thought school was more important than anything else. They quizzed Derek before tests and helped him study. Derek cared about school, too.

Later, a reporter visited his childhood home. One wall was covered with sports and school awards for Derek and Sharlee. When the reporter asked Derek which award meant the most to him, he pointed to a math certificate. He worked really hard for it, he said.

The Jeters had lots of family discussions, too, about right and wrong, and being respectful. Derek's parents were loving, but strict.

Once, Derek refused to shake hands with a kid on an opposing team. His dad gave him a lecture. That wasn't being a good sport. Playing baseball wasn't just about winning. Derek never did something like that again. Later, his dad coached Derek's team and was even tougher. Charles didn't just give him the shortstop position. Derek had to earn it.

So Derek practiced, practiced, practiced. He

worked hard at everything he did. Still, by the time Derek was thirteen years old, he had yet to beat his dad at any game.

One day, he challenged his dad to a game of one-on-one basketball. Derek hustled. He nailed his shots. And he won! It meant a lot to Derek . . . and to Charles. He couldn't have been prouder.

Derek's childhood sounds ideal. But it wasn't. Not always. Kalamazoo was a small city of around 220,000 people. "Sometimes you felt the stares," Derek said. "If you go somewhere with your mother, you're a little bit darker. You go somewhere with your dad, you're a little lighter."

People called him names, from "Oreo cookie" to "zebra" to worse. But Derek tried not to let it get to him. When someone asked him his color, he just answered, "black-and-white."

Derek had lots of friends. He was popular with boys and girls, and even teachers. They liked the way he worked hard and the respectful way he treated everyone.

But Derek wasn't perfect. He talked and joked around—a lot! He even got "unsatisfactory" in conduct on his report cards.

Derek went to St. Augustine's through eighth grade. It was a small Catholic school. When he graduated, his class put out a yearbook. In it, everybody imagined they were having a ten-year reunion. Derek's section read: "Derek Jeter, a professional ballplayer for the Yankees, is coming around. You've seen him in grocery stores, on the Wheaties box, of course."

Derek did wind up on Wheaties boxes. He even had his own cereal, Jeter's Frosted Flakes. But that was in the future. First, Derek had to make his high-school team.

Chapter 3
High-School Challenges

Derek wanted to go to Kalamazoo Central. It was, after all, right in his backyard. His best friends were going there, too. Central was big. One thousand students attended the three-story brick building.

Charles and Dot wanted Derek to go to a Catholic high school. They knew Derek wanted to play high-school basketball, as well as baseball. The Catholic school was smaller. Derek had a better chance of making both teams there.

Derek was not going to give in easily. He made a deal with his mother. That summer he was going to try out for a really good summer basketball team called the Kalamazoo Blues.

If he made the team, his mom agreed he could go to Central.

During tryouts for the Blues, Derek won every running drill. When other boys said they were too tired to keep practicing, Derek said he was ready for more.

He made the team.

The summer passed with Derek playing basketball—and baseball, too, of course. Then, just before Derek started Central, his parents sat him down for a talk.

His parents explained what they expected of Derek for high school. They had a contract for him to sign.

They talked about grades, about girls, and about sports. They came up with a set of rules. Some were simple, like "Eat your lunch!" Others were harder: No baseball if he failed a class. No baseball if he smoked, drank, or did drugs. His dad felt this was especially important. Charles was a substance-abuse counselor. He helped people who had problems with drugs and alcohol. He'd seen firsthand what could happen to teenagers.

It all made sense to Derek. He was scared to do that stuff anyway. He knew it was bad for his body—and bad for his game. Besides, he wanted to make his parents proud. Sharlee had a different view. "Derek was a wimp," she joked later.

Derek signed the contract. He was ready for high school.

He made the Central basketball team and played all winter. Then, one cold February day, baseball tryouts were called. Derek headed to the gym with the other freshmen. The junior varsity coach was in charge.

"JV" teams are younger, with less experience than varsity. Varsity teams have the best players.

The coach hit some balls to the freshmen. Derek caught one, then fired it to first base.

The throw was so strong, the coach called in the
varsity coach.

The varsity coach liked what he saw. But
Derek didn't make varsity, at least not right away.

For most of the season, he stayed on JV. Then the senior shortstop agreed to step aside. He knew Derek was the better player. "As long as you keep batting me third," the senior told the coach, "that's fine."

Derek moved up. He was on high-school varsity, at only fourteen!

That summer he joined a high-level baseball team called the Maroons. The team played about seventy-five games, with little time to practice. In snowy Michigan, athletes could only play outdoors a few months of the year. Derek wanted to make every minute of summer count. So he came early to games. He stayed late. As long as someone would pitch or hit to him, he'd stay to practice.

All through high school, Derek played
basketball and baseball. Keeping to his contract,
he studied hard. He worked as a tutor in the
computer lab. He also found time for fun. He went
to parties. He had a girlfriend. She remembered
when they first met in eighth grade. It was easy.
Derek was the one in the Yankees jacket.

After school, Derek's friends would come
over. They'd listen to music or watch TV, while

Derek practiced on an indoor batting machine in the garage. He took about one thousand swings every day.

By his senior year, Derek had grown to be 6'3" He was still skinny, all arms and legs. Even so, he had a great arm. He threw balls ninety-three miles per hour and was a natural base runner, with a batting average of over .500 every year. And he had the attention of baseball scouts from across the country.

BASEBALL SCOUTS

BASEBALL SCOUTS, LIKE SCOUTS FOR ANY SPORT, SEARCH FOR THE BEST NEW ATHLETES. THEY DRIVE AND FLY ALL OVER THE COUNTRY AND ALL OVER THE WORLD TO SEE YOUNG PLAYERS COMPETE IN GAMES. THEIR JOB: TO REPORT BACK TO THEIR BALL CLUB ON EACH PLAYER'S SKILL, DRIVE, AND ABILITY. THEIR OPINIONS CAN MAKE OR BREAK A PLAYER'S FUTURE—AND THE TEAM'S SUCCESS.

Some scouts worked for colleges, and some were from major league teams. But they all went to Derek's games and kept track of his stats.

Derek homered in the first two games of the season. For the next two, Central faced their crosstown rivals in a doubleheader. Of course Derek wanted to win. He always wanted to win.

But he wanted to impress the scouts, too. More than forty had come to watch. He snuck a look at the scouts. Some held radar guns. Some had stopwatches. They all wanted to clock his speed.

In the first game, Derek started with a home run. But he struck out his next at bat. Derek didn't know it, but that would be his only strikeout for the season. Still, his team lost 12–8.

After that loss, Derek felt he had to try even harder in the second game.

In the first inning, Derek hit a slow ball to the infield. He raced for first, hoping to beat the throw. But there was still snow on the ground. The base was wet and slippery. Derek stumbled, twisting his ankle. In pain, he hopped around, afraid to look down.

The crowd fell silent. Derek's dad helped him off the field. What if he had broken his ankle? Derek wondered. He'd be out for the season.

Luckily, it was a sprain. But it was a severe one. Doctors said he'd have to miss most of the season.

Four games later, Derek was back as a designated hitter. He wore an ankle brace and high-top cleats. He hobbled from base to base.

And he couldn't hit the ball as hard as he could before.

Amazingly, he finished the year with a .508 batting average and twenty-three RBIs. ("RBI" stands for *runs batted in*. A player is awarded one when he brings in a run because of a hit or a walk.) He was at the top of every scout's list.

Now Derek had decisions to make. The Major League Baseball draft was coming up. Would he go to college or turn pro?

THE MAJOR LEAGUE DRAFT

THE DRAFT IS A SYSTEM, A WAY FOR TEAMS TO CHOOSE NEW PLAYERS FROM HIGH SCHOOLS AND COLLEGES. ALL THIRTY BALL CLUBS ARE ON THE SAME PHONE CALL, LISTENING AND TALKING, AS EACH TEAM GETS A TURN TO PICK. THE TEAM WITH THE WORST STANDING FROM THE YEAR BEFORE GOES FIRST. THE TEAM WITH THE SECOND-WORST STANDING GOES NEXT, AND SO ON. EACH TEAM GETS A SET NUMBER OF MINUTES TO CHOOSE A PLAYER, UNTIL ALL THE TEAMS HAVE USED UP THEIR PICKS.

Chapter 4
Waiting and Wondering

The night before the draft, Derek didn't fall asleep until 4:00 a.m.

Derek knew which teams had the first five picks. He knew the Yankees went later. No way would he get to play for New York, he thought. He expected to be one of the first players chosen. He felt so sure, he didn't even know which team chose sixth.

June 1 was the big day. Across the country, each team met on its own. Everything was done over the phone. The draft wasn't televised.

The Houston Astros went first. Their scout wanted Derek to be an Astro. But the team chose a college player instead. The scout felt it was such a big mistake, he quit his job.

Teams two and three, the Indians and the Expos, took pitchers. The fourth team to pick was Baltimore. They had the premier shortstop in the league, Cal Ripken Jr. They didn't need another. So they didn't pick Derek. Cincinnati, the fifth team, also had an all-star shortstop. The team went with an outfielder.

CAL RIPKEN JR.

The first five teams were done, and Derek hadn't been chosen. Derek wasn't a major leaguer. And he had no idea what would happen next.

Meanwhile, a cheer rang out in the Yankees draft room. Derek's dream team had the number six pick! And Derek Jeter was still on the list!

A Yankees official made the call. They'd take Derek Jeter of Kalamazoo Central.

In Kalamazoo, a local sports reporter heard the news first. He called Derek right away. "I can't believe it!" Derek shouted. "I just can't believe it!"

Of course, one phone call didn't make Derek Jeter a New York Yankee. He had to sign a contract, and that took time. Everyone had to agree on a salary. And what about college? Education was important to Derek's parents—and to Derek, too. They talked it over with Yankees officials. And the Yankees agreed to pay for Derek's college, whenever he decided to go.

When all was said and done, the Yankees' offer was too good to turn down.

On June 28, two days after he turned eighteen, Derek's dream came true: He became a New York Yankee.

Chapter 5
On His Own

Now Derek had a contract with the Yankees. Did that mean he'd be putting on pinstripes and playing in Yankee Stadium? No! That was the major leagues. Like all the other new players, Derek would have to prove himself in the minors first, with teams owned by the Yankees organization.

By now, Derek was two weeks late for Rookie League play in Tampa, Florida. So he had to get ready quickly. He felt terrible saying good-bye to Sharlee. She'd be starting high school soon. Leaving his family was just about the hardest part of playing baseball. Derek boarded the plane to Florida "with a lump the size of a golf ball in my throat."

THE MINORS

MINOR LEAGUE (OR "FARM") TEAMS FIRST FORMED THE NATIONAL ASSOCIATION OF PROFESSIONAL BASEBALL LEAGUES IN 1901 AND PLAYED ORGANIZED GAMES. EVENTUALLY, THESE LOW-LEVEL TEAMS JOINED MAJOR LEAGUE TEAMS TO "FEED" PLAYERS INTO THEIR HIGH-LEVEL CLUBS. ALSO CALLED PLAYER DEVELOPMENT PROGRAMS, MINOR LEAGUE TEAMS TRAIN ATHLETES FOR THE MAJORS. AS PLAYERS IMPROVE, THEY MOVE UP TO THE NEXT LEVEL, USUALLY IN THIS ORDER:

- ROOKIE LEAGUE
- CLASS A
- CLASS AA, OR DOUBLE A
- CLASS AAA, OR TRIPLE A
- AND FINALLY, THE MAJORS!

In Tampa, everyone already had a roommate. Derek felt like an outsider.

Derek was alone in a strange city, barely eighteen. It was hard getting used to everything—even baseball. Derek went 0 for 7 in his first game. After a week, he still hadn't had a hit.

For the first time, Derek wondered if he'd be good enough to make it.

He called home throughout the day and sometimes in the middle of the night. Almost always, he was in tears. His parents were so worried, they flew to see him twice in six weeks.

Derek felt lost.

But he didn't show it. He kept calm on the field and with his teammates. Slowly, he made progress.

In the fall, he went to the University of Michigan. Then in the spring of 1993, it was back to baseball for his first full season as a pro.

Derek was heading to Class A in the minor leagues. One more step on the way to the majors.

Chapter 6
Taking on the Minors

In Class A baseball, in Greensboro, North Carolina, Derek bonded with teammates. He had fun playing. He was named Most Outstanding Major League Prospect by the South Atlantic League managers. Still, he made fifty-six errors.

All along Derek had been planning to go back to college in the fall. But baseball was his future. And he knew he needed more training. So after the season, when the Yankees wanted him to stay on for extra instruction, he put college on hold.

The hard work paid off. Usually, the Yankees didn't promote players once a season began. But in 1994, Derek moved from Class A to AA to AAA.

He wasn't that lost, crying boy anymore.
He was making friends like Jorge Posada and
Mariano Rivera. He was playing hard in the field
and getting hits. At the end of the season, he was
named Minor League Player of the Year by *USA
Today* and other newspapers.

In 1995, living in Tampa during the off-season, Derek kept training and improving. In April, he returned to his Triple A team in Columbus, Ohio. Then, on May 28, at 6:00 a.m., there was a knock on his hotel room door. It was the team manager. Yankees shortstop Tony Fernandez had pulled a muscle. "You're going to the big leagues," the manager told Derek.

Derek flew to Seattle that morning for a series against the Mariners. In the locker room, he got his first Yankees uniform. On the back was his number: 2.

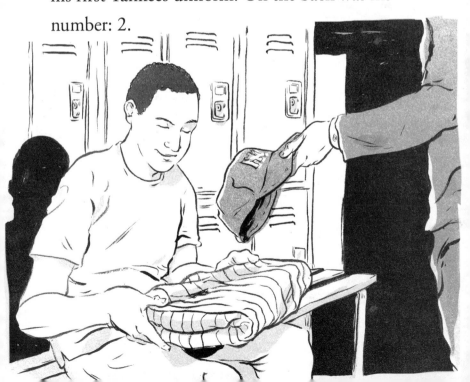

UNIFORM NUMBERS

IN 1929, THE YANKEES WERE THE FIRST TEAM TO USE UNIFORM NUMBERS, TO HELP FANS KEEP TRACK OF PLAYERS. BY THE 1930S, ALL MAJOR LEAGUE TEAMS HAD THEM. AT FIRST, YANKEES' NUMBERS WERE ASSIGNED BASED ON BATTING ORDER. IF A PLAYER HIT THIRD IN THE LINEUP, LIKE BABE RUTH, HE GOT NUMBER 3. SOME TEAMS MATCHED NUMBER WITH POSITION. THEN CAME ANOTHER SYSTEM: THE LOWER THE NUMBER, THE HIGHER THE PLAYER'S IMPORTANCE TO THE TEAM. AS FOR DEREK HIMSELF, #2 JUST HAPPENED TO BE AVAILABLE FOR HIS DEBUT.

Derek ran onto the field with the rest of the team. He couldn't believe it. He was sharing the infield with all-stars captain Don Mattingly and Wade Boggs!

He looked for his dad in the stands. And sure enough, Charles was there. His mom had stayed in Kalamazoo for Sharlee's high-school softball game. Derek understood. His parents had two children. Not just one.

The first game, Derek went 0 for 5. But the next day, he singled. His first major league hit! His dad was so excited, he jumped out of his seat.

Mostly, Derek felt relief. He'd gotten over the first hurdle in the majors.

Derek played in fifteen games, including some

at Yankee Stadium. He listened to coaches and players. He worked hard. Everyone liked him— even other shortstops who were trying for the position.

"Although he was taking your job, you were still pulling for him," one player said. "He was such a nice guy."

Things were really working out for Derek. The Yankees were flying to Detroit, Michigan, for their next road trip, and he couldn't wait.

About a hundred people from Kalamazoo came to Tiger Stadium to cheer him on.

Derek, only twenty, felt like a pretty big deal. But standing by his locker he heard the news: Fernandez was off the disabled list. Derek was off the roster, and back down to Triple A.

Friends and family wouldn't see him wearing the Yankees pinstripes, after all. Even worse, he was demoted.

"Don't worry about it," Mattingly told Derek. "You'll be back."

Chapter 7
Starting at Short

The next year, 1996, Derek *was* back as the Yankees' starting shortstop.

Once, Derek tried to steal third. Instead, he made the third out. Derek knew he was in trouble. But in the dugout, he sat right next to Joe Torre, the manager. He was ready to take the punishment from "Mr. Torre," as he called him. But Torre just rubbed his head and told him to get lost. He figured Derek

JOE TORRE

already knew he'd made a big mistake. Torre didn't need to rub it in.

But Derek wanted to take responsibility. He spoke to reporters about the error. While he never spoke about his personal life, or said anything against players or coaches, he always owned up to mistakes.

Like any baseball season, Derek's first had its ups and downs. After one poor performance, a

Chicago newspaper called him "shortslop." He came back the next day, feeling just as confident. By the end of the season, he was named Rookie of the Year.

In early September, Derek invited his dad to his Detroit hotel room.

It wasn't to discuss baseball. He told him he had an idea: to start a charity foundation,

like his favorite Yankee,
Dave Winfield. The David
M. Winfield Foundation
helped families in need.

Derek knew kids
looked up to major league
players. And he wanted
to be a role model. It
was the beginning of
the Turn 2 Foundation.

DAVE WINFIELD

Its goal: to keep kids off alcohol and drugs. Derek
wanted to help kids become leaders.

And he helped the Yankees make their first postseason appearance since 1981.

Derek was only twenty-two years old. During the regular season, he'd been relaxed. Could he keep his cool now?

In Game One, Derek left six men on base when he made outs at bat. The Yankees lost. "All I can do is forget about it," Derek told reporters.

Before he left the stadium, Derek poked his head into Torre's office. "Make sure you get your sleep tonight. Tomorrow is the most important game of your life," Derek joked. He knew that's what Torre wanted to say to *him*! Even under pressure, Derek was kidding around.

The next day Derek scored the winning run in the twelfth inning. He made the tying run in another game, and got on base to keep the Yankees going in the next.

Derek and the Yankees took the series!

Next, for the American League Championship,

the Yankees faced the Baltimore Orioles. A lot hinged on Game One, a home game for the Yankees.

In the eighth inning, the Yankees were down 4–3, with one out. Derek, at bat, hit a fastball. The ball soared toward the right-field wall. The Oriole outfielder got in place. He thought he could make the play. But twelve-year-old Jeffrey Maier reached over and caught the ball.

No interference, ruled the ump. It was a home run! Derek circled the bases, tying the score. The Yankees wound up winning in eleven innings.

The call made headline news. Was it right or wrong? Derek admitted he had a little help. But he thought everything would have turned out the same, with the Yankees taking the pennant. After all, they had pitching greats Andy Pettitte and David Cone, plus star batters Bernie Williams and Paul O'Neill.

And now Derek and the Yankees were heading to the World Series.

Chapter 8
World Series Magic

The Braves ruled. They were World Series Champions in 1995—and were heavily favored to win in 1996. The Yankees were the underdogs—the team that had to beat the odds to win.

For Derek, the stakes were higher than ever. He wanted to keep enjoying playing baseball. But he was dead serious about winning.

The Yankees lost the first two games. But time and again, Derek came through to start a rally. The momentum swung to the Yankees. They began to win. Then, at 10:56 p.m., on October 26, the last Braves batter popped out. The Yankees were World Series champs. Finally!

Derek threw his arms in the air. He joined his

teammates for a pileup on the pitcher's mound,
then a victory lap around the stadium.

"It's just magic," he said in the clubhouse.

The celebration continued three days later at the victory parade in New York City.

One city official estimated that close to three million people came out to cheer, more than for any other championship parade. "The extra million was for Jeter," Yankees player (and New York Mets star) Darryl Strawberry said.

Young fans skipped school to hold up signs saying "We played hooky to see our rookie." Other signs read "Marry me, Derek" and "No. 2, be my No. 1."

Derek was a fan favorite. With his good looks and easygoing personality, he was popular with men and women—young and old, black and white. "I think I can relate to everyone," he's said.

Later on in Michigan, three thousand people squeezed into Derek's old gym at Kalamazoo Central for a Jeter Day celebration. Sharlee gave a speech. She said she wasn't Derek's fan because of baseball. It was because he was such a great brother.

Derek was embarrassed by the attention. But winning the championship was an amazing feeling. He wanted that feeling every season. He got it in 1998 and 1999, when the Yankees won back-to-back World Series.

In 1998, Derek led the American League with 127 runs scored. He was leading the team, too—on and off the field—to a record-breaking 125 wins. Some consider the '98 Yankees the best team in baseball—ever. Their 125 wins in one season is still a Major League Baseball record.

Derek didn't let it go to his head. "If I ever want to go home again, I can't change," he said. He still hung out with old friends. He liked being in the middle of a big group of people. But he didn't have wild nights on the town like other celebrity athletes.

He liked to stay home and watch movies and ESPN, too. He was a regular guy who did his own laundry and drove himself to ball games. On the field, he still looked to make sure his parents were there. He still hustled like a rookie. He was, in fact, called "the most low-maintenance star" by team officials. He joked around with teammates. He signed autographs. He talked to kids in the stands. If they were near the batting circle during warm-up, he'd ask what they thought: Should he swing on the first pitch?

He was a good guy, a good guy who always wanted to win. And when the Yankees reached the 2000 World Series, he wanted it more than ever. They were facing their crosstown rivals, the New York Mets.

Excitement swept through the entire city. Derek lived in New York for part of each year. Everyone knew him. If he lost, he would never hear the end of it.

Every game turned out to be a nail-biter. The Yankees took the first two, the Mets the third. It seemed the next game might go their way, too.

But Derek Jeter led off Game Four. He swung on the very first pitch.

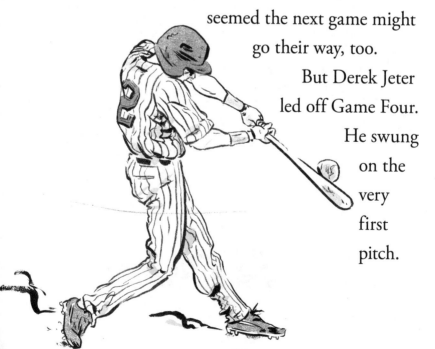

SUBWAY SERIES

THE 2000 WORLD SERIES WAS A SUBWAY SERIES: A MAJOR LEAGUE SERIES PLAYED AT TWO BALLPARKS CONNECTED BY A SUBWAY SYSTEM. FANS CAN TAKE SUBWAY TRAINS TO BOTH FIELDS. THAT YEAR, GAMES WERE SPLIT BETWEEN SHEA STADIUM IN QUEENS AND YANKEE STADIUM IN THE BRONX.

The ball flew into the bleachers. A leadoff home run! The Yankees won that game and the Series. "Every time . . . we got it going," the Mets general manager said later, "Jeter did something to change the game."

Derek won World Series MVP, capping a year where he'd already won the All-Star MVP award. He was the leader of the new Yankees dynasty, and living his dream.

Chapter 9
Tragedy and Triumph

Derek Jeter should have been on top of the world. At the start of the 2001 season, he was just twenty-six years old. He already had four World Series rings. He earned more than almost every baseball player. He had dated lots of celebrities, from superstar singer Mariah Carey to Miss Universe.

MARIAH CAREY

But that same year, Sharlee was being treated for cancer. Sharlee and Derek had always been close, talking on the phone each day. Now they talked on the phone in the middle of the night, too.

Derek kept playing. He didn't tell many people about Sharlee until the end of May, when doctors said she was cancer-free. The next day, Derek hit a three-run homer. The next day was Mother's Day, and Sharlee and Dot and Charles were cheering from the stands.

Then came more devastation: September 11,
when terrorists flew planes into New York's World
Trade Center. Thousands died.

Derek and his teammates did what they could
to help. They visited victims in hospitals. They
spent time with children who lost parents. Derek
wasn't doing it to make news or for people to say
what a great guy he was. In fact, he told reporters
to stay away. Some things shouldn't be in the
newspapers, he felt. These visits were private.

New Yorkers, stunned and sad, told Derek they wanted the Yankees to win another title for the city. Derek was going to do his best to give it to them.

In the American League Division Series, the Yankees were pitted against the Oakland Athletics. Down two games to one, hopes were fading. In the eighth inning of Game Four, they clung to a 1–0 lead.

Oakland was at bat, with two outs and a man on first. The batter smashed a long drive into the right-field corner. A double! Could the runner on first make it home?

Yankees outfielder Shane Spencer made the throw to infield. Two cutoff men stood along the first-base line. Their job: to get the ball home. But Spencer threw it over both their heads.

The A's thought they had an easy run, and a tie score. They were wrong.

Out of nowhere, Derek raced for the ball. He scooped it up on just one bounce, using both hands.

Still running, he flipped the ball sideways—right on target. Jorge Posada caught it at home and easily tagged the runner.

"What was he even doing in that spot?" one Oakland player wondered. But Derek was there. He made the "flip," still considered one of the best defense plays in baseball history. Derek would only say he was doing what he was supposed to be doing. Helping the Yankees win.

He hoped he could do the same in the World Series, playing against the Arizona Diamondbacks.

By Game Four, the Diamondbacks were ahead, two games to one. Derek came up to bat in the tenth inning with the score tied. Leaving the dugout he said, "This game is over." Teammates said he wasn't bragging. That wasn't Derek's way. He just knew something had to be done.

His World Series batting average flashed on the screen. A very low .067. It was midnight now, November 1. After 9/11, baseball had been put on hold. So now for the first time, the World Series continued past October.

Meanwhile, Derek kept his at bat going, struggling to stay at the plate. At 12:04, he connected for a hit. But not just any hit. The ball sailed over the right-field wall for a home run. A fan held up a sign: *Mr. November.* And the nickname stuck. The Yankees won,

and took the series to a full seven games. But the final game ended in a victory for Arizona.

Derek was crushed. For him, losing the World Series meant a losing year. And while he led the Yankees to strong seasons in the years that followed, the Yankees had stopped winning championships.

Still, Derek had personal achievements, with All-Star appearances and awards. In 2003, he was named Yankees captain, the first since Mattingly retired in 1995. The Yankees always waited for the right man to lead the team. And now it was Derek.

Teammates said Derek was a quiet leader. He guided by example. And when he had something upsetting to say? He always took the player aside. He never called anyone out in front of a group. And of course he was still a sports superstar. But like any pro athlete, he struggled at times, too.

In 2004, Derek had a major batting slump: one hit in thirty-six at bats. When he came to the plate on April 29, fans still rose to their feet. On the first pitch, he broke the slump with a home run.

That same year, ace shortstop Alex Rodriguez joined the Yankees. "A-Rod" was the American League MVP. Some thought he had stronger skills than Derek.

ALEX RODRIGUEZ

That he'd be named shortstop. But Derek, the heart and soul of the team, stayed on. In July, everyone understood why.

Derek dove face-first into the stands to catch a Red Sox pop fly. He stopped a twelfth-inning rally right then and there. No one worked harder than Derek Jeter.

In 2008, Derek was asked to make a speech after the last game in Yankee Stadium. The team was moving to a new ballpark across the street. But the old park held strong memories for Derek.

Running through the clubhouse tunnel on the way to the field before every game, he'd always tap one sign for luck. The sign had a quote by Joe DiMaggio: "I want to thank the Good Lord for making me a Yankee."

Derek felt the same way. That night, the Yankees' captain explained his feelings to the crowd. He thanked the fans, saying, "We just want to take this moment to salute you." He took off his cap. He also took home the Joe DiMaggio sign.

In the new stadium the very next year, the Yankees won their twenty-seventh World Series. Derek had the most hits of any player.

And at the new Yankee Stadium, in 2011, Derek stepped up to the plate for another historic at bat. Two years earlier, he'd broken the Yankees' batting record with his 2,722nd hit. But now Derek's batting stats were low. They were the worst of his career. Still, the fans cheered. It was a beautiful summer day. And Derek Jeter only needed two hits to become the first Yankee to reach 3,000.

He hit a double for number 2,999.

When Derek came up to bat again, he didn't care if he got a single, double, or triple. He just didn't want a "slow roller to third base, and have that replayed forever." No one thought he'd homer. He only had two so far that season.

On their feet, fans chanted, "Der-ek Je-ter. Der-ek Je-ter." The Yankees and the opposing Rays stood by their dugouts. On the eighth pitch, Derek swung. The ball flew over left-center field.

"That ball's outta here!" one Yankees coach shouted.

A home run! Derek ran quickly. The first baseman took off his cap to Derek as he passed. The other Rays clapped in the field. Derek's teammates were waiting at home plate. When Derek touched base, the crowd roared.

That day, Derek went five for five. He was the twenty-eighth player to reach 3,000 hits, and only the second to do it with a home run. It was over, Derek thought. Now he could get back to being Derek Jeter.

Chapter 10
A New Chapter

In 2012, the Yankees reached the American League Championship Series. In the twelfth inning of Game One, Derek dove for a grounder. His left ankle twisted as he fell.

It was broken.

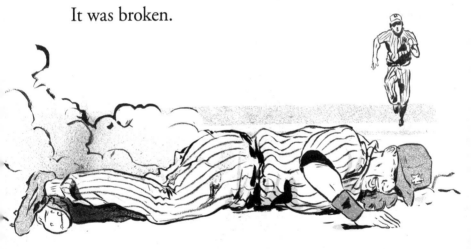

Derek was out for the Series. And without Derek, the Tigers swept the Yankees.

It was a long recovery. Derek missed the first few months of the 2013 season. Then came more injuries. Every other season, Derek had played about 150 games. That year he played seventeen.

Derek was turning forty. Clearly, he was slowing down. He used the time off to think. He was still playing shortstop, a position that required energy and razor-sharp skills.

Baseball had always been fun. No matter how hard he worked, it had never seemed like a job. Now, for the first time, it did.

On February 12, 2014, Derek posted on his Facebook page, "The 2014 season will be my last year playing professional baseball."

Derek Jeter was retiring.

For over two decades, Derek had lived and breathed baseball. He didn't marry. He didn't finish college. In the post, Derek talked about how he gave his all for the sport. How he wanted time now. Time to start a family. See the world. Have a summer vacation. "I have gotten the very most out of my life playing baseball," he wrote, "and I have absolutely no regrets."

What would he do next? In his last season, Derek started Jeter Publishing, with a plan to publish all sorts of books, sports books included. There's still work to be done with Turn 2, helping Sharlee, who's president. And who knows? There might be another World Series ring in Derek's future. This time, as an owner. "That's the next goal," he told a reporter. "Calling the shots."

Meanwhile, the 2014 season became Derek's farewell to baseball. One New York newspaper ran a "this day in Jeter history" for every date. Teams honored Derek when he played at their ballparks.

When the Mets and Yankees played, the Mets gave Derek a $22,222.22 check for Turn 2, and a New York City subway tile mosaic.

In Oakland, the video tribute did *not* include Derek's famous "flip" play. That was okay with Derek. "I'm sure they've all seen it," he said.

The tributes went on and on. At the end of the season, the Yankees honored their captain by wearing Derek Jeter patches. Their last home game, on September 25, was declared Derek Jeter Day. That night it was supposed to rain.

There was a chance the historic game would be postponed. But the skies stayed clear.

Derek admitted he felt nervous. The Yankees were done for the season. Everything and everyone would be focused on him. He was so rattled, he forgot to put on his elbow guard for an at bat. Yet once again, Derek came through.

In the bottom of the ninth, with the score tied, Derek stepped up to the plate. It was his last at bat at Yankee Stadium. Ever.

He drove the ball into right field for a single, bringing the runner home and winning the game. In seconds, Derek was mobbed by teammates.

The opposing Orioles stood and cheered. The fans had been cheering all night long, chanting, "Thank you, Derek."

At the end, Derek said he didn't need to be thanked. He was just doing his job. It was the fans who should be thanked.

Now the Jeter era is over. The man who's been

called "Jetes," "DJ," "Captain Clutch," and "Mr. November" is retired. But he won't be forgotten.

Derek was a player who stuck with the Yankees through thick and thin . . . who never considered changing teams for money . . . who tried, always, to do the right thing.

He was a player who had fun playing baseball . . . who rarely got angry . . . who, no matter how many games he played, still looked for his parents in the stands . . . who made his teammates better . . . and who never stopped trying.

"For those who say today's game can't produce legendary players," the late Yankees owner George Steinbrenner once said, "I have two words: Derek Jeter."

TIMELINE OF
DEREK JETER'S LIFE

1974 —— Derek Sanderson Jeter is born, June 26th, in Pequannock, New Jersey

1980 —— Goes to first Yankee game

1988 —— Makes high-school varsity baseball team as a freshman

1992 —— Graduates from high school, is drafted by the Yankees

1995 —— Makes major league debut on May 29th, against Seattle Mariners

1996 —— Named Yankees starting shortstop
Wins Rookie of the Year Award
First World Series win

1998 —— First All-Star appearance

2000 —— Named MVP of the All-Star Game and World Series MVP

2001 —— Makes "flip play" against Oakland A's in the playoffs
Nicknamed "Mr. November" in the World Series against Arizona Diamondbacks

2003 —— Named Yankees captain

2004 —— Wins first Gold Glove Award

2006 —— Wins first Silver Slugger Award

2011 —— Homers for his 3,000th hit

2014 —— Makes fourteenth and last All-Star appearance
Becomes #6 on list of all-time hits leaders
Retires

TIMELINE OF
THE WORLD

37th US president Richard Nixon resigns from office	1974
US hockey Olympic team upsets rival Soviet Union team to win gold	1980
US boycotts Moscow summer Olympics to protest Soviet Union invasion of Afghanistan	
NBA adds expansion teams Miami Heat and Charlotte Hornets	1988
New York City temperature is 88 degrees on 8/8/88	
Euro Disney opens outside Paris	1992
The DVD is developed and named for "digital versatile disc" or more commonly, "digital video disc"	1995
Google is launched	1998
Nelson Mandela steps down as president of South Africa	1999
Hillary Clinton is elected to the US Senate while still First Lady	2000
9/11: terrorists fly planes into New York City's World Trade Center and the Pentagon near Washington, DC	2001
The last old-fashioned Volkswagen Beetle is built	2003
Ireland is the first country to ban smoking in all workplaces	2004
Liberia's Ellen Johnson Sirleaf becomes the first female leader in all of Africa	2006
A series of 355 tornadoes hits 21 states from April 25 to 28, the largest outbreak in US history	2011
Children's book authors Walter Dean Myers (*Fallen Angels*), Eric Hill (Spot the Dog picture books), and Sue Townsend (*The Secret Diary of Adrian Mole*) pass away	2014

BIBLIOGRAPHY

* Craig, Robert. **Derek Jeter: A Biography**. New York: Pocket Books, Simon & Schuster, 1999.

Jeter, Derek, with Jack Curry. **The Life You Imagine**. New York: Crown Publishers, 2000.

* Jeter, Derek, edited by Kristen Kiser. **Game Day: My Life On and Off the Field**. New York: Three Rivers Press, Crown Publishers, 2001.

The New York Times, introduction by Tyler Kepner. **Derek Jeter: From the Pages of The New York Times**. New York: Abrams, 2011.

O'Connor, Ian. **The Captain: The Journey of Derek Jeter**. Boston; New York: Houghton Mifflin Harcourt, 2011.

* Stout, Glenn and Matt Christopher. **On the Field with Derek Jeter**. New York: Little, Brown and Company, 2000.

* Books for young readers